FAITH STRONGER THAN DEATH is a book about adjustment; about how to help yourself and others during times of bereavement. Drawing upon personal experience, Jim Towns has written a brief unique guide to survival and strength during times of greatest emotional stress. He undertands and deals with the anger, the questions, the fears and uncertainties that plague all who ever lost a loved one.

He answers the "whys" of death; traces the normal grief process; reveals the solace of the Scriptures; asks and answers the most significant questions about death, and suggests additional readings for those who desire them.

DEDICATION

THIS BOOK IS PRESENTED

IN

GRATITUDE TO GOD FOR HIS LOVE AND GRACE

IN

APPRECIATION TO MY FAMILY AND FRIENDS

FOR THEIR UNDERSTANDING

AND IN

MEMORY OF A LOVELY LADY
WHO LIVED FOR OTHERS,
AND PAID THE PRICE FOR MY
KNOWLEDGE CONCERNING GRIEF:

MONA HANCOCK TOWNS

FAITH STRONGER THAN DEATH!

HOW TO COMMUNICATE EFFECTIVELY
WITH A PERSON IN GRIEF

James E. Towns, Ph. D.

WARNER PRESS ANDERSON, INDIANA

FAITH STRONGER THAN DEATH!

A PORTAL BOOK
Published by Pyramid Publications for Warner Press, Inc.

Portal edition published June, 1975

Copyright © 1975 by Warner Press, Inc.
All Rights Reserved

ISBN: 0-87162-182-7

Printed in the United States of America

PORTAL BOOKS are published by Warner Press, Inc.
1200 East Fifth Street, Anderson, Indiana 46011, U.S.A.

CONTENTS

ACKNOWLEDGMENTS	8
PREFACE	9
QUESTION 1. WHY?!	13
Laws of Nature	15
Human Imperfection	16
Community Living	17
Divine Impartiality	18
QUESTION 2. WHAT IS THE NORMAL GRIEF PROCESS?	21
Shock	22
Emotion-Weeping	23
Panic	24
Depression	25
Physical Distress	26
Guilt	27
Repression	28
Resentment	29
Hope-Acceptance	29
QUESTION 3. WHAT DOES GOD'S WORD SAY ABOUT DEATH?	31
God's Promises Based On His Word	33
Strength	33
Peace	34
Comfort	35
Grace	36
Position	36
Sovereignty	37
Victory	39

QUESTION 4. WHAT ARE THE MOST SIGNIFICANT QUESTIONS ASKED ABOUT DEATH?   43

WHAT BASIC KNOWLEDGE SHOULD I HAVE CONCERNING WHAT TO DO WHEN DEATH OCCURS? WHOM SHOULD I CALL?   43

IS THERE SOMEONE WHO CAN HELP ME GET MY BUSINESS AFFAIRS IN PROPER ORDER?   45

HOW CAN I PREPARE FOR DEATH?   50

I AM A CHRISTIAN, BUT I DO NOT UNDERSTAND WHY I DO NOT HAVE JOY AND PEACE IN MY LIFE. HOW CAN I HAVE A MEANINGFUL SPIRIT-FILLED LIFE HERE ON EARTH?   65

WHAT IS THE DIFFERENCE IN THE WAY A CHRISTIAN AND A NON-CHRISTIAN MEET DEATH?   74

WHAT CAN I SAY TO SOMEONE IN GRIEF?   75

WHERE ARE THE DEAD RIGHT NOW AND WHAT ARE THEY DOING?   76

HOW DO I TELL CHILDREN ABOUT DEATH?   78

WHAT ABOUT A DEFINITE TERMINAL ILLNESS?   80

WHERE CAN I FIND HELP IN
THE BIBLE WHEN I HAVE A
TIME OF NEED? 81

CONCLUSION 85
DIAGRAM OF GRIEF PROCESS 89
DEFINITION OF TERMS 91
SUGGESTED READING 95

ACKNOWLEDGMENTS

No one ever writes a book alone, whatever the title page may assert. I am deeply indebted to individuals with whom I have come in contact and whose ideas have slipped unconsciously into my lifestyle and may have surfaced here as my own. I have been as careful as possible to give credit, but so many individuals have helped me that I could never acknowledge all the influences.

I am grateful to the following friends who read all or part of this book in manuscript form: Bill Austin, Joyce Brown, Ralph Busby, John Butts, Ben Dickerson, Karolene Inman, George Loutherback, and Dave Petty. Their thoughtful suggestions and criticisms were valuable in helping me to see what I was doing and saying.

Special appreciation is expressed to Rosanne Enmon for typing the manuscript.

PREFACE

This book had to be written! In the last five years I have been deeply acquainted with death and grief. In a short span of time I lost my mother, two grandparents, an uncle and aunt, five members of my chapter of Theta Chi Fraternity, and several friends. Students in my classes at the university are frequently absent due to a death in their family or friends.

In my early grief, I treated my thoughts and feelings as if they were abnormal. Soon I learned that regardless of how strong the Christian faith a person has, it is normal to have disturbing feelings during the process of grief. As I began to understand sorrow, I have been trying to help people who are bereaved to profit from my new insights. Each time I go to be with a family in sorrow, I want to be able to present them with a brief, power-packed book that will help them to understand their normal grief behavior. This is why this book had to be written. It is for those who are in grief and those who need to understand sorrow in order to help a relative or friend.

Writers have always had difficulty using the confining tool of words to describe ideas, attitudes, and concepts. My purpose is to attempt to put in words some helpful hints from the Christian perspective concerning how to effectively communicate with yourself and others about the normal grief process.

This book is written for those who personify Mark 9:24: "Lord, I believe; help my unbelief." It is designed to try to explain the logic of the Christian faith concerning death.

Many times when a tragedy occurs, people tend to harshly blame God for that which has happened. This book presents the scriptural perspective of man as a free moral agent interacting with God's natural law and sovereignty. It is a practical statement about how to respond in the process of normal grief.

Take a look at grief. If you have known it, you will remember. If you have not lost someone you love, then imagine yourself suddenly alone in an alien world. Your body is weary, your emotions are raw. Your heartache is a real physical ache. You are convinced that your life is destroyed. You do not know how to think, how to stop feeling, how to start feeling, what to do and what not to do. Knowledge cannot erase our emotions which accompany sorrow, but knowledge can help us guide ourselves and each other toward recovery.

Our contemporary society has no time for death. A death is usually handled quickly and is rapidly forgotten by most people. Yet grief remains. The great complicated task is how to accept the breakup of family unity and function under the high pressure and fast pace of life today in such a way that grief does not destroy the survivors.

This book is about adjustment. If you have no interest in helping yourself and others, then this is not for you. This is not a complex theological, philosophical work, but a simple direct statement of behavior while one is in bereavement.

There are several places that people search for answers to grief: philosophy, psychology, sociology, and science. Please do not misunderstand, all these are good if they are used appropriately. However, if I am honest, I must use my intellectual integrity and give the Christian faith an opportunity to work in my life.

If my readers are to be open, they are given the freedom to accept or reject some behavior principles based on God's Word. This book is launched with the prayer that many may learn to treat their normal grief behavior in a normal way.

If these ideas stimulate questions and discussion and provide some answers, they will have served a meaningful purpose. If you will think, plan, and prepare to accept grief and sorrow as a part of life, perhaps you will avoid the dangerous trend of treating your normal grief behavior as if it were abnormal.

Jim Towns
Department of Communication
Stephen F. Austin State University
Nacogdoches, Texas

Question 1
WHY ?!

Death is the strongest force known to most people. Paul Tillich pointed out that every person always lives in the conscious or unconscious anxiety of having to die. Death may come at any time. There is never a time when we should be surprised, yet there seldom seems to be a "right" time for dying.

The subject of death is a taboo topic for many people. In spite of this, it is a matter of individual concern. Although most people do not want to talk about it, they do desire to know more about how to deal with the grief process.

The first time I experienced death in my immediate family resulted in a lingering, slow adjustment to a new normal life. If I had known then what I now know about the normal grief process, I would have mourned, of course, but I would have been aware of what was happening to me. I would have known how to respond to my bewildering emotions and what to expect from my normal psychological behavior. There were so many unanswered questions and feelings. It is normal to ask the question "Why?"

At first I turned to logic to provide my answers for why the death happened. It is inevitable that all men die. It was my thinking that if I could have reasons or purposes for things happening, then I could better accept them. This line of thinking yielded the idea that suffering and tragedy are not caused by "gross and terrible sins that we have committed" nor just "the judgmental will of God." God does not randomly and impersonally will tragedy upon us. If we trust Him, He is the God of love who is there to take care of us in all aspects of life and death. Many times we blame God for something that we could have possibly brought on ourselves.

Scripture teaches that sorrow and suffering in the world are the direct and indirect result of sin. The one word that best describes the consequences of sin is *death*. Sin is the breaking of God's law. In other words, it is anything that interferes with our having an adequate relationship with God through Jesus Christ.

Breaking God's law carries the death penalty. He said to Adam and Eve: "In the day that thou eatest thereof [the tree of the knowledge of good and evil] thou shalt surely die" (Gen. 2:17). Paul summed it up in these words: "The wages of sin is death" (Rom. 6:23).

There are two kinds of death. Both are the results of sin. Physical death is the transition or separation of body and spirit. This death results in the decay of the body (Eccles. 12:7). The death of the physical body is part of the penalty of sin. If there had not been any sin, there would have been no physical death. Adam and Eve would not have died had they not sinned. From that day to this, death has been in the world. The Christian will experience only physical death.

Spiritual death is the separation of the spirit from God. This death results in the ruin of the spirit. "Them that know not God . . . shall be punished with everlasting destruction from the presence of the Lord, and from the glory of his power" (2 Thess. 1:8-9). Just as spiritual birth is more glorious than physical birth, the spiritual death is more terrible than the physical death.

In order to answer any questions about physical and spiritual death that you may have, refer to Chapter Four concerning the question, "How Can I Prepare For Death?"

Since sin and death came into the world, it seems that there are four logical reasons for suffering and tragedy today. They are: (1) laws of nature, (2) human imperfection, (3) community living, and (4) divine impartiality.

Laws of Nature

There are natural indiscriminating laws of nature. God set natural law into motion. If we accept the assets of nature—beauty, wealth, and so on—then we must accept the liabilities of nature also—disease, tornados, floods, earthquakes, and so on.

Disease is one of the laws of nature. There are no simple answers for why some people contract diseases and others never seem to be sick. God does not *make* people get sick, nor does he indiscriminately will disease on a person. If we scorn God, then we have an inadequate theology or concept of who God is and how He works.

The material environment which God has provided finds its stability in the fact that it is law-abiding. The rain may aid one set of human purposes and harm another. It may seem that the world and environment are cruel and hopeless, but there is a stability.

God does not always heal the diseased physical

body. A Christian doctor related that he prays for healing—if it is God's will. He never tells patients that one will be physically healed if he has enough faith. People who say that God always heals if one has enough faith are strangely inconsistent. They wear false teeth, glasses, and other artificial aids. In the Bible there is a principle which could be called the "economy of the miraculous." God seldom works a miracle when there is a normal way available, and He does not always intervene when the case is medically hopeless.

Human Imperfection

Man is a frail framework. He can not always see that which is best or right in ultimate terms. Man makes decisions and must live with the consequences whether good or bad. Many times people blame God for accidents or mistakes. The real reasons are due to human imperfection.

A plane crash in a storm may point out human imperfection in man's decision-making processes. The pilot or his superiors saw the storm. They could have gone around it or over it or turned back. But they decided that it would be all right to go through it. But the raging storm was worse than they had anticipated. Something dreadful happened. No one knows for sure. The tragic plane crash came as a result of human imperfection in reasoning concerning what to do about the approaching storm.

Accidents are usually a result of someone's imperfect reasoning. The automobile accident could have been avoided if the drivers had been responsible and considerate of each other. When automobiles go fast enough to provide reasonable transportation, they also go fast enough to maim or kill.

Disease may result from imperfect reasoning. We reason that the food is delicious as we gorge ourselves.

Perhaps in our diets there are elements that react against the physical body and certain types of unexplained diseases find their beginnings. Some processed food products may not be healthy.

Perhaps we did not do the right thing at the right time in order to avoid becoming ill. We may not have sought proper medical attention at the proper time. It is our imperfect reasoning powers that get us into problems. Most of the time we are asking why God does not do something to help us in these matters, and He is probably wondering why we do not do more with our knowledge and ability.

Community Living

We do not live to ourselves in this world. As population explodes we realize that what one person does has an effect on others. When one person gets the flu, usually many people get it. Epidemics take their toll.

When one person does something out of order then usually the bystanders are affected. In other words, because we live and function in groups of people, many times one person may be responsible for another person's death.

In 1966 a young man climbed to the top of the tower on the University of Texas campus. He pulled out a gun and began shooting at students in all directions. Then the man shot himself. Because he lived in a community, Charles Whitman not only hurt himself with a gun at the University of Texas tower, he also hurt twenty-one other people. If Whitman had been on a deserted island it would have been a different story. But he was in a community of people and his actions hurt many innocent people.

In community living, tragedies may result if people are not responsible and considerate of each other. In our contemporary society the misuse of alcohol and drugs has taken an overwhelming toll in harming people. Many innocent people have been harmed by another person who is under the influence of drugs.

It seems so senseless, but many times the actions of others bring harm or death to innocent bystanders.

Divine Impartiality

"Good" comes to good people and bad people. "Bad" comes to good people and bad people. It rains on the just and the unjust.

Think about the example of the two houses and foundations of sand and rock (Matt. 7:24-27). The storms, rain, and wind came to both houses. They did not just come to the house on sand. The house on the rock stood—but it did go through the storm. I sometimes think that although it stood, the house probably had to be reshingled, repapered, and repainted. But it did stand. If the foundation of a person's life is God's Word, he will be standing during and after the storm.

When I was in deep sorrow, going through a storm, doubts flooded my mind. At a major crisis point, the following statement of commitment was made:

> As I walk the way of inquiry which has produced doubt, uncertainty, and rank skepticism, I'm not afraid to entrust an unknown immediate future to my known God.
>
> So many things have happened that could make my actions be based on superstition, but I'm not afraid to entrust an unknown immediate future to my known God.
>
> I've endeavored in many seemingly worthwhile activities but have produced few visible affirmative results, but I'm not afraid to entrust my unknown immediate future to my known God.

When I question "Why?" I realize that God wants me to know. "My little child, if you could see it the way I see it, you would not worry; you would know that I am taking care of you in a very ultimate, special way." I'm not afraid to entrust an unknown immediate future to my known God.

Perhaps due to some of these previously mentioned factors, we have been a victim of the natural indiscriminatory laws of nature, human imperfection, community living, and divine impartiality.

Later on, I became aware that the grumbling that I was doing toward the situation and my unanswered questions were not against the situation; they were against God!

In the situations which occur in life I feel that God must be thinking: "I must be faithful to man. He is trusting himself, friends, family, and society rather than Me. Man must trust Me." To be sensible in life's situations is to be dependent on God. In order to understand and adjust, a Christian must think like God thinks. It is through His Word that we learn how He thinks. Man must respond: "Thank you, Lord, you are in charge" (1 Thess. 5:18).

God is sovereign. The devil could not accuse man until God permitted him to do so. In the book of Job, chapters 38-40, Job asked why all the sorrow and grief came to him. He tried to tell God that there was a better way to do things. Job thought he was wise. Then God asked Job some questions which proved His Providence and sovereignty. When Job realized who God was and more about His plans, he responded to God by saying, "I do not know everything. How could I ever find the answers? I lay my hand upon my mouth in silence. I have said too much already."

Some of the answers to my "whys?" or unanswerable questions have been revealed in the fact that God dared to show me what a sinful man I am and that which still lies in my subconscious. He permitted the "darkness" or "storm" to come. But he also continued to work. I must stop asking for answers to unanswerable questions and thank God for the life and work of the deceased.

Question 2
WHAT IS THE NORMAL GRIEF PROCESS?

One of the major reasons that most people have trouble adjusting to someone's death is that they do not understand the normal grief process. They treat their normal behavior as if it were very abnormal. This compounds problems. Many people do not understand adjustments simply because they have never been confronted with the issues. They never thought to prepare or to expend effort to understand the normal grief process.

Death is ever-present; thus, adjustment to death is ever-present. Despite the inevitability of death, it seems that bereavement is usually unexpected and is accompanied by a process of grief.

It does not make any difference how brave and strong we are or think we can be. We must call grief or sorrow by its right name in order to comprehend it for what it is. We should not, by any reflection or twist of words we use, minimize what we are going through when death removes a member of our family or a friend.

A fact remains: someone we loved is deceased; this person is no longer with us. We are human and we miss that person.

Grief is the process of readjusting to our environment from which the deceased is missing and start forming new relationships. In other words, it is a series of thoughts, feelings, and actions during a period of adjustment to the loss of a loved one. Most people are inadequate within themselves to cope with all the crisis situations surrounding death. Perhaps death is usually more difficult for the family than for the one who dies.

When death occurs, there are several stages of grief for the survivors who mourn. Each individual does not necessarily go through all the stages, nor does he necessarily go through the stages in the order in which they are presented here. Sometimes it is difficult to differentiate between each of the stages. But, as Granger Westberg's writings (ideas here are used by permission) point out, the normal grief process may include shock, emotion-weeping, panic, depression, physical distress, guilt, resentment, repression, and hope.

Shock

Shock is a blow, impact, sudden agitation of the mental or emotional sensibilities. It is a numbing, anesthetized reaction we may experience immediately upon hearing about the death of someone we love.

Shock may last a few minutes, hours, or days. If it goes on for weeks then it becomes unhealthy. Do not be afraid of the shock that occurs at first. On several occasions when I have learned of the death of someone dear to me, I was stunned! I walked around in almost a trance or daze. I heard people talking to me, but the words did not register. I was numb.

Shock is a temporary escape from reality. Shock is also the body's natural way of protection and God's provision or gift to endure grief for a while. After a few hours or days we must face the reality of the loss. One of the best things to do for someone in shock is to keep that person fairly busy carrying on as much usual activity as possible during the crisis time. The sooner the individual has to deal with immediate problems and make decisions, the better. This may seem hard, but otherwise the person could lose a great deal of self-confidence and contact with reality. We should be near and available to help, but do not hinder the therapeutic value of the person doing what he can do for himself.

A person may come and go in a state of shock. When I have been in shock I sometimes found myself saying, "I cannot believe this really happened." I knew that it did happen, but I could not accept it emotionally.

There is not only a mental shock, but also a social shock. A married person is suddenly a single person. It is a social shock to have to function in society without the spouse.

Emotion-Weeping

Emotions cannot be separated from situations or experiences which evoke them. Emotion is an inside thermometer which is affected by outside events. When a person is in grief, weeping is an expression of deep inner feelings. The first step in dealing with weeping is to realize the fact that it is an emotion and that it is God's way of helping us to relieve inner pressure.

Our emotions come when it begins to dawn upon us what we have lost. It is normal that for many people their emotions well up with an uncontrollable urge to express their grief. The most healthy thing to do is to allow ourselves to weep and express the emotions we actually feel.

In the American society it is difficult for some men

to cry. They have been taught from the moment they put on their first pair of boots that little boys do not cry. Therefore, many men think that weeping is a sign of weakness. If they tense up and refuse to express their emotions, they may be in for trouble. The expression of emotions is essential to most people. To try to repress emotions is to make them less than human.

I am not talking about "emotionalism." One of the faults of many "spiritual robots" is that their perspective has tended to stifle the expression of sorrow upon the death of a loved one. We should encourage the expression of grief. Sometimes people are embarrassed to sorrow or weep openly. If this is the case, they should be by themselves and let their sorrow take its natural course. We should not keep emotions bottled up within ourselves; there are a number of ways by which we may release them. Express them to yourself, to a friend, or to someone who you know cares for you. There is truth in the idea that a joy shared doubles it; a sorrow shared halves it. This may not be a once-for-all happening. It is normal to continue to weep at times about your loss for a year or two. Significant days concerning the deceased are hard to face—days such as birthdays, Mother's Day, anniversary of the death date, and so on.

Panic

Panic is a sudden, severe, overpowering fright. When we become confronted or obsessed with our loss, in some instances we become panicky because we can think of nothing but the loss. When I am in the grief process, it seems that my mind can go only a few seconds without thinking about my loss. The inability to concentrate is normal and natural during the grief process.

It is the fear of the unknown or fear of something that we do not understand that causes us to panic. Therefore, it is important that people understand something about the grief process in advance of their loss so they will not treat this normal behavior as if it were abnormal. This kind of knowledge can eliminate part of the panic.

The first time I experienced the grief process and was in deep sorrow, I did not know what to expect. I thought that my life was a wreck because of the feelings that flooded me. I began to panic; I thought that I might even be losing my mind because I could not control my feelings, thoughts, and words.

Gloom soon surrounds panic. Oftentimes it is natural to want to be alone. However, we must not linger in our gloom because this will extend our adjustment time. It is a comfort to understand that even panic is a normal reaction to a stressful situation such as death. Panic may soon evolve into depression.

Depression

In the normal grief process many people may eventually feel depressed. This is the saddening and lowering of our mental spirit. It is an extreme difficulty or burden. In other words, it is the emotional state of dejection or despair and feelings of worthlessness and apprehension.

When we find ourselves in the depth of depression or despair we begin to feel that no one has ever had a loss as significant as ours. Then something seems to come between ourselves and us, family, friends, and even God. When this happens we find ourselves thinking thoughts that we would never otherwise have ventured. At one point in my deep sorrow, I felt that no one cared. I did not think that even God cared. I knew that he could have kept the death from happening if he would have wanted, but he did not. And I was angry. It is easy to develop a "persecution complex" when we are depressed.

Depression comes to most people when someone they love is taken away from them. One of the most beneficial things we can do for someone depressed by grief is to stand by in quiet confidence and assure him or her that "this too shall pass." The bereaved will probably not understand you at first. As the length and intensity of the depression lessens, the person has a fuller appreciation for those who are standing by.

For some people the depression clouds seem to roll away. For others it may take weeks and months before any new rays of light break through. If depression is prolonged it is highly possible that physical and mental distress will occur.

Physical Distress

Physical distress is the endurance of physical pain and symptoms of illness due to the grief process. Many people become physically ill because of an unresolved grief situation. They have not worked through the problems relating to the death. Unless a person somehow can resolve their emotional problems relative to the normal grief process, then that person may possibly become physically ill. Notice I said "resolve," not "solve." We must resolve ourselves into acceptance and adjustment.

One of the major causes of illness during the grief process is that "as a man thinketh, so is he." The hard, depressing emotions of a person's mind and personality can make his body physically sick. Some of the physical symptoms of distress during the grief process may be: (1) feeling tightness in the throat, (2) choking with shortness of breath, (3) need for sighing, (4) empty feeling in the abdomen, (5) lack of muscular power, and (6) an intensive distress described as tension. When a person is in the grief process his night dream world may be affected with horrible dreams about the situation or death of the deceased. These dreams may emotionally drain a person for hours or days. This kind of physical and mental distress is normal. When a person feels distress and sorrow, he may start feeling guilty about some of the factors in the grief process.

Guilt

Normal guilt is a feeling of having committed a breach of conduct. Guilt comes when we do not meet what we expect of ourselves as well as what others expect of us. Neurotic guilt is feeling guilty out of proportion to the real involvement in the particular problem.

Guilt feelings often come when we feel that we should have been there to do or suggest something that may have been of some comfort or assistance to the deceased.

Guilt feelings may come when we realize that we did not treat the deceased in the appropriate manner. 1 John 1:9 is a good prescription for guilt. It affirms that if we confess, God is faithful to forgive and cleanse. Guilt and misunderstanding of emotions makes us feel miserable for a long time. We must not be afraid to talk about our feelings of guilt with those who care for us.

Often there is a feeling that responsibility to the loved one has not been properly taken care of while the person was alive. Sometimes there is a basis for this, but on many occasions, this may not be true. Whatever the reason for feelings of guilt, it should be realized that it is normal to feel guilty because we could not make our situation better. When we cannot make the situation or conditions better, then resentment or repression occurs.

Repression

Repression is a defense behavior by which an individual prevents painful thoughts and desires from entering his conscious mind. In other words, it is "selective forgetting." The thoughts are not really forgotten. They keep coming back to the conscious mind.

Repressed feelings continue to influence behavior. Oftentimes the person is unaware of the real basis for some of his thoughts, beliefs, and actions. A new painful experience may trigger a flood of many repressed feelings. If a person is trying to repress his feelings about the death of a loved one, and he suddenly sees a funeral procession, he may break into tears. He could not continue to repress the painful feelings that were bottled up inside.

Repressed feelings or thoughts may be very active and may find an outlet in dreams when the conscious mind lowers its controls. When a person is under continued frustration, repressed thoughts may increase in strength and threaten to break through into the conscious mind and even into overt actions.

Threats of mentally painful experiences lead to the arousal of anxiety and additional defenses. Repression is self-deception. It is much better to be realistic and work through the painful thoughts rather than to be evasive. Repression takes considerable mental energy which is then not available for direct attempts to resolve the problems of life.

Many times when repressed feelings are allowed to come into the conscious mind, resentment may spring up. If resentment is not adequately treated immediately then many problems may arise.

Resentment

Resentment is the feeling of indignant displeasure because of something regarded as wrong. In our depression, strong feelings of hostility and resentment may rise.

Many who are in the grief process go through a time of being very critical of everything and everyone who was related to the loss. As one tries to understand why the death happened, he tends to blame others. He expresses resentment to anyone who cared for the deceased. No matter what was done on behalf of the deceased, he feels that it was insufficient.

This type of resentment gives rise to a question like "Why did God let this happen?" Remember, there are laws of nature, human imperfection, community living, and divine impartiality. At times a person becomes so desperate in his resentment that he cannot live with himself, much less with anyone else. Resentment hurts oneself more than anyone else.

It is comforting to know that all this behavior is normal in the grief process. In spite of resentment and all other emotions, there is hope.

Hope-Acceptance

Hope is expectation toward obtaining a comfortable new normal life. We need to express our emotions. We need encouragement from others. Some people take an attitude of shutting out possibilities for a new and meaningful normal life. Notice that I did not say possibilities for the old and meaningful normal life again. The past is gone. Life will never again be the same as we knew it with our loved one. But there can be a *new* normal life.

When I experienced deep sorrow in the grief process for the first time, I felt that I would never be happy again. Nothing could ever ease the heartache. I did not know that it was normal to feel that way for a while. Only in acceptance lies hope. There is no hope and peace in forgetting, in resignation, or in busyness. Acceptance is the key. You may ask, "But how do I accept something that I don't want to accept?" Are you willing to be willing to let go of your selfish motives and trust God in His sovereignty? If the answer is "no," then keep praying for a willingness to be willing.

God is never weary with our new beginnings. Ask God for thoughts of mind and impressions of heart as you accept His ultimate sovereign plan for your life. The Bible tells of many men and women who have taken God at his word and trusted. God does not always grant us our wants, desires, and wishes, but He does meet our needs. Many times I get the definitions of these words mixed up. I think that a desire or wish or want is a *need*. God meets our real needs as we trust him. Jesus comes to us at the point of our need and shows that his word will give us meaning and purpose in life.

People of faith do not suddenly get that way. The Christian grieves deeply over his loss and goes through the grief process. Eventually we understand that everything has not been taken from us and we want to live again.

Hope and reality are based on faith in God's Word. Though we continue to struggle, we do find a new normal life. The struggle is hard if we try to do it on our own. Relax, take God at His Word, regardless of how you feel.

In the next chapter we will become aware of what God's Word will do for us while we are in the grief process.

Question 3
WHAT DOES GOD'S WORD SAY ABOUT DEATH?

My first experience in the grief process resulted in despair. Many people tried to help by giving me books to read. I was disillusioned with the standard books concerning death. Some friends even suggested that I read certain selected scriptures in the Bible. At one point my sorrow was so deep that I was tempted to never look at a Bible again because I was mad at God.

If you feel cold toward reading the Bible and this reflects your attitude also, then we can empathize through this chapter as I reveal that it was my inadequate concepts of God that made me not want to read His Word. I was not "willing to be willing" to be open to God and let His Word change my perspective. An important question comes to you now—Are you willing to be willing to give God's Word a chance to change your heart and mind and give you the comfort that you need so desperately right now? Whether the answer is yes or no, I want to present a challenge. Start each day of your life with a brief prayer: "Lord Jesus, please make yourself better known to me. Fill my life. Take charge of it and use it as you see fit." If you really mean that prayer, some incredibly wonderful things will happen to you!

I discovered that the Bible reveals much about people who have had the same needs that I now have!

Perhaps by now you are thinking, It sounds good, but I have heard that kind of thing before and it always turns out to be the same old cold experience when I read the Bible. Let me assure you that I am aware of this problem. I suggest that you ask God to help you to reject your feelings and by faith take him at his word. Mark 9:24 states it perfectly: "Lord, I believe; help my unbelief."

When I rejected my feelings and began to trust the Lord by faith, my reading of the Bible changed my old perspective. I now avowedly accept the Bible as the authoritative Word of God which presents the standard of faith and practice. It is the revelation of God's actions with his people throughout the ages, particularly through Jesus Christ.

The Bible contains the truths, prophecies, and a message of hope to man which could not have been the mere product of human minds. There are truths set forth in the Scripture which men could never have known if those truths had not been divinely revealed. The fulfillment of prophecy bears witness to the inspiration of the Bible. The message of the Scripture attests its inspiration. It tells us the kind of God we have. It reveals the awful nature and consequence of sin. It points out the way of salvation and the real purpose of life.

These scriptures are presented with full assurance that God's word will not return void, but will accomplish what he pleases in your life. The selections are from the Living Bible and other translations.*

God's Promises Based On His Word

Keep in mind, whether anticipated or unanticipated, the death of a loved one may cause both Christian and non-Christian to go through a grief process in adjustment to their loss. The Christian makes his adjustment by making his daily experience synonymous with his position in Christ. In other words, the Christian should make his daily activities and perspective consistent with the will of God for the Christian life according to the Bible.

When I was in the different stages of the grief process (shock, weeping, panic, depression, physical distress, guilt, resentment, and repression) I did not even try to employ God's Word in my daily life. I was too busy feeling sorry for myself concerning my loss. As I continued in a deep sadness, I began to despair. It was at this point that I became desperate enough to try reading the Bible.

Strength

When I became willing to be willing to be open to God's Word, I found out it really works! I felt so weak and inadequate and I needed strength.

Isaiah 40:28-31

Don't you yet understand? Don't you know by now that the everlasting God, the Creator of the farthest parts of the earth, never grows faint or weary? No one can fathom the depths of his understanding. He gives power to the tired and worn out, and strength to the weak. Even the youths shall be exhausted and the

---

*Selections from *The Living Bible* used by permission of Tyndale House Publishers, Wheaton, Illinois.

young men will all give up. But they that wait upon the Lord shall renew their strength. They shall mount up with wings like eagles; they shall run and not be weary; they shall walk and not faint.

2 Corinthians 12:9

My grace is sufficient for you, for My power is made perfect in your weakness.

Peace

The more selfish I became during the grief process, the less peace I had in my life. Scripture gives explicit statements concerning how to obtain the peace that we so desperately need.

Romans 5:1-6

So now, since we have been made right in God's sight by faith in his promises, we can have real peace with him because of what Jesus Christ our Lord has done for us. For because of our faith, he has brought us into this place of highest privilege where we now stand, and we confidently and joyfully look forward to actually becoming all that God has had in mind for us to be.

We can rejoice, too, when we run into problems and trials for we know that they are good for us—they help us learn to be patient, and patience develops strength of character in us and helps us trust God more each time we use it until finally our hope and faith are strong and steady. Then, when that happens, we are able to hold our heads high no matter what happens and know that all is well, for we know how dearly God loves us, and we feel this warm love everywhere within us because God has given us the Holy Spirit to fill our hearts with his love.

When we were utterly helpless with no way of escape, Christ came at just the right time and died for us sinners who had no use for him.

Philippians 4:4-7
Always be full of joy in the Lord; I say it again, rejoice! Let everyone see that you are unselfish and considerate in all you do. Remember that the Lord is coming soon. Don't worry about anything; instead, pray about everything; tell God your needs and don't forget to thank him for his answers. If you do this you will experience God's peace, which is far more wonderful than the human mind can understand. His peace will keep your thoughts and your hearts quiet and at rest as you trust in Christ Jesus.

Isaiah 26:3
He will keep in perfect peace all those who trust in him, whose thoughts turn often to the Lord.

Philippians 4:7
The peace of God, which surpasses all understanding, will keep your hearts and minds in Jesus Christ.

John 14:27
Peace I leave with you; my peace I give to you; not as the world gives do I give to you. Let not your hearts be troubled, neither let them be afraid.

Comfort

Closely connected to the need for peace was the need for comfort.

John 14:1-4
Let not your heart be troubled. You are trusting God, now trust in me. There are many homes up there where my Father lives, and I am going to prepare them for your coming. When everything is ready, then I will come and get you, so that you can always be with me where I am. If this weren't so, I would tell you plainly. And you know where I am going and how to get there.

Handwritten notes at top:
- 1st Time I saw Katy W. - hospital room - 10 yr. ago
- couple mo. ago → wept - didn't want to leave - LIKE Jesus
- concerned about family → John 14:1 → "don't let hearts be tr.
- "Why?" - God knows about dying.

As I started trusting God, I began to learn more about his loving kindness and grace. In God's grace, we are given a position with him.

Grace

2 Corinthians 12:8-10

Three different times I begged God to make me well again.

Each time he said, "No. But I am with you; that is all you need. My power shows up best in weak people." Now I am glad to boast about how weak I am; I am glad to be a living demonstration of Christ's power, instead of showing off my own power and abilities. Since I know it is all for Christ's good, I am quite happy about "the thorn," and about insults and hardships, persecutions and difficulties; for when I am weak, then I am strong—the less I have, the more I depend on him.

Position

1 Thessalonians 4:13-18

And now, dear brothers, I want you to know what happens to a Christian when he dies so that when it happens, you will not be full of sorrow, as those are who have no hope. For since we believe that Jesus died and then came back to life again, we can also believe that when Jesus returns, God will bring back with him all the Christians who have died.

I can tell you this directly from the Lord: that we who are still living when the Lord returns will not rise to meet him ahead of those who are in their graves. For the Lord himself will come down from heaven with a mighty shout and with the soul-stirring cry of the archangel and the great trumpet-call of God. And the believers who are dead will be the first to rise to meet the Lord. Then we who are still alive and remain on the earth will be caught up with them in the clouds to meet the Lord in the air and remain with him forever. So comfort and encourage each other with this news.

2 Corinthians 5:1-10

For we know that when this tent we live in now is taken down—when we die and leave these bodies—we will have wonderful new bodies in heaven, homes that will be ours forevermore, made for us by God himself, and not by human hands. How weary we grow of our present bodies. That is why we look forward eagerly to the day when we shall have heavenly bodies which we shall put on like new clothes. For we shall not be merely spirits without bodies. These earthly bodies make us groan and sigh, but we wouldn't like to think of dying and having no bodies at all. We want to slip into our new bodies so that these dying bodies will, as it were, be swallowed up by everlasting life. This is what God has prepared for us and, as a guarantee, he has given us his Holy Spirit.

Now we look forward with confidence to our heavenly bodies, realizing that every moment we spend in these earthly bodies is time spent away from our eternal home in heaven with Jesus. We know these things are true by believing, not by seeing. And we are not afraid, but are quite content to die, for then we will be at home with the Lord. So our aim is to please him always in everything we do, whether we are here in this body or away from this body and with him in heaven. For we must all stand before Christ to be judged and have our lives laid bare—before him. Each of us will receive whatever he deserves for the good or bad things he has done in his earthly body.

Sovereignty

As I came to a deeper understanding of the Christian's position, then I began to have a better comprehension of God's sovereignty.

37

Romans 8:22-39

For we know that even the things of nature, like animals and plants, suffer in sickness and death as they await this great event. And even we Christians, although we have the Holy Spirit within us as a foretaste of future glory, also groan to be released from pain and suffering. We, too, wait anxiously for that day when God will give us our full rights as his children, including the new bodies he has promised us—bodies that will never be sick again and will never die.

We are saved by trusting. And trusting means looking forward to getting something we don't yet have—for a man who already has something doesn't need to hope and trust that he will get it. But if we must keep trusting God for something that hasn't happened yet, it teaches us to wait patiently and confidently.

And in the same way—by our faith—the Holy Spirit helps us with our daily problems and in our praying. For we don't even know what we should pray for, nor how to pray as we should; but the Holy Spirit prays for us with such feelings that it cannot be expressed in words. And the Father who knows all hearts knows, of course, what the Spirit is saying as he pleads for us in harmony with God's own will. And we know that all that happens to us is working for our good if we love God and are fitting into his plans.

For from the very beginning God decided that those who came to him—and all along he knew who would—should become like his Son, so that his Son would be the First, with many brothers. And having chosen us, he called us to come to him; and when we came, he declared us "not guilty," filled us with Christ's goodness, gave us right standing with himself, and promised us his glory.

What can we ever say to such wonderful things as these? If God is on our side, who can ever be against us? Since he did not spare even his own Son for us but gave him up for us all, won't he also surely give us everything else?

Who dares accuse us whom God has chosen for his own? Will God? No. He is the one who has forgiven us and given us right standing with himself.

Who then will condemn us? Will Christ? *No!* For he is the one who died for us and came back to life again for us and is sitting at the place of highest honor next to God, pleading for us there in heaven.

Who then can ever keep Christ's love from us? When we have trouble or calamity, when we are hunted down or destroyed, is it because he doesn't love us anymore? And if we are hungry, or penniless, or in danger, or threatened with death, has God deserted us?

No, for the Scriptures tell us that for his sake we must be ready to face death at every moment of the day—we are like sheep awaiting slaughter; but despite all this, overwhelming victory is ours through Christ who loved us enough to die for us.

For I am convinced that nothing can ever separate us from his love. Death can't, and life can't. The angels won't, and all the powers of hell itself cannot keep God's love away. Our fears for today, our worries about tomorrow, or where we are—high above the sky, or in the deepest ocean—nothing will ever be able to separate us from the love of God demonstrated by our Lord Jesus Christ when he died for us.

Victory

At one point in my grief, I felt that my life was a wreck and that I would be a complete failure because my sorrow had robbed me of any victory in adjustment. The scripture pointed out how I could find the victory that I so badly needed.

1 Corinthians 15:1-4, 19-28, 35-58

Now let me remind you, brothers, of what the Gospel really is, for it has not changed—it is the same Good News I preached to you before. You welcomed it then and still do now, for your faith is squarely built upon this wonderful message; and it is this Good News that saves you if you still firmly believe it, unless of course you never really believed it in the first place.

I passed on to you right from the first what had been told to me, that Christ died for our sins just as the Scriptures said he would, and that he was buried, and that three days afterwards he arose from the grave just as the prophets foretold . . .

And if being a Christian is of value to us only now in this life, we are the most miserable of creatures.

But the fact is that Christ did actually rise from the dead, and has become the first of millions who will come back to life again some day.

Death came into the world because of what one man (Adam) did, and it is because of what this other man (Christ) has done that now there is the resurrection from the dead. Everyone dies because all of us are related to Adam, being members of his sinful race, and wherever there is sin, death results. But all who are related to Christ will rise again. Each, however, in his own turn: Christ rose first; then when Christ comes back, all his people will become alive again.

After that the end will come when he will turn the kingdom over to God the Father, having put down all enemies of every kind. For Christ will be King until he has defeated all his enemies, including the last enemy—death. This too must be defeated and ended. For the rule and authority over all things has been given to Christ by His Father; except, of course, Christ does not rule over the Father himself, who gave him this power to rule. When Christ has finally won the battle against all his enemies, then he, the Son of God, will put himself also under his Father's orders, so that God who has given him the victory over everything else will be utterly supreme. . . .

But someone may ask, "How will the dead be brought back to life again? What kind of bodies will they have?" What a foolish question! You will find the answer in your own garden! When you put a seed into the ground it doesn't grow into a plant unless it "dies" first. And when the green shoot comes up out of the seed, it is very different from the seed you first planted. For all you put into the ground is a dry little seed of wheat, or whatever it is you are planting, then God gives it a beautiful new body—just the kind he wants it to have; a different kind of plant grows from each kind of seed. And just as there are different kinds of seeds and plants, so also there are different kinds of flesh. Humans, animals, fish, and birds are all different.

The angels in heaven have bodies far different from ours, and the beauty and the glory of their bodies is different from the beauty and the glory of ours. The sun has one kind of glory while the moon and stars have another kind. And the stars differ from each other in their beauty and brightness.

In the same way, our earthly bodies which die and decay are different from the bodies we shall have when we come back to life again, for they will never die. The bodies we have now embarrass us for they become sick and die; but they will be full of glory when we come back to life again. Yes, they are weak, dying bodies now, but when we live again they will be full of strength. They are just human bodies at death, but when they come back to life they will be superhuman bodies. For just as there are natural, human bodies, there are also supernatural, spiritual bodies.

The Scriptures tell us that the first man, Adam, was given a natural, human body, but Christ is more than that, for he was life-giving Spirit.

First, then, we have these human bodies and later on God gives us spiritual, heavenly bodies. Adam was made from the dust of the earth, but Christ came from heaven above. Every human being has a body just like Adam's, made of dust, but all who become Christ's will have the same kind of body as his—a body from heaven. Just as each of us now has a body like Adam's, so we shall some day have a body like Christ's.

I tell you this, my brothers: an earthly body made of flesh and blood cannot get into God's kingdom. These perishable bodies of ours are not the right kind to live forever. But I am telling you this strange and wonderful secret: we shall not all die, but we shall all be given new bodies! It will all happen in a moment, in the twinkling of an eye, when the last trumpet is blown. For there will be a trumpet blast from the sky and all the Christians who have died will suddenly become alive, with new bodies that will never, never die; and then we who are still alive shall suddenly have new bodies too. For our earthly bodies, the ones we have now that can die, must be transformed into heavenly bodies that cannot perish but will live forever.

When this happens, then at last this Scripture will come true—"Death is swallowed up in victory." O death, where then your victory? Where then your sting? For sin—the sting that causes death—will all be gone; and the law, which reveals our sins, will no longer be our judge. How we thank God for all of this! It is he who makes us victorious through Jesus Christ our Lord!

So, my dear brothers, since future victory is sure, be strong and steady, always abounding in the Lord's work, for you know that nothing you do for the Lord is ever wasted as it would be if there were no resurrection.

Read and believe scripture. It tells you about the goodness of God and the immortality of the soul. As you trust the Bible, you will find a deep conviction welling up in your mind that his words are true indeed!

Question 4

WHAT ARE THE MOST SIGNIFICANT QUESTIONS ASKED ABOUT DEATH?

QUESTION ONE

> *What basic knowledge should I have concerning what to do when a death occurs? Whom should I call?*

Sometime, a relative or friend may turn to you in time of bereavement. You will be faced with new and sudden responsibilities. There will be many unfamiliar things which you must take care of—at once! Any death creates an emergency situation for the family. In this emotional crisis you will probably need to contact these people to help make arrangements:

1. *Attending physician or medical examiner.* If a doctor was attending the deceased, he will help you start making arrangements. If the death was the result of violence or could have been the result of a criminal

act, the medical examiner must examine the circumstances. The police will help you with many details.

2. *Funeral director*. Contact a funeral director whom you respect. He will advise you and guide you in your selections. You should feel no embarrassment in discussing with him your desires and ability to pay. He should be helpful in making suitable arrangements that are "right" for the family.

The funeral director should secure necessary burial permits and death certificates. He will counsel with you regarding the funeral plans. He will place obituary and funeral notices in the newspapers which you desire and will also contact radio stations, if appropriate.

If the deceased is to be taken to a distant point for burial, the funeral director will make the necessary arrangements.

It is the funeral director's job to assist you in every way to make the funeral a memorial service that is an expression of your faith.

3. *The minister*. The minister will offer comfort to the family and make himself available to all who need special counseling. He will help you to set up the order of the funeral service. Ask the minister to conduct a Christian memorial victory service based on God's Word rather than conducting a sad funeral.

The minister will collaborate closely with the funeral director in planning the details of the service at the church and at the grave site.

4. *Family and friends*. You may need to call members of the family and close friends and inform them of the death that has occurred. Ask others to aid in making the many calls that must be made.

Feel free to ask others to help in meeting the needs

of those in grief. Everyone close will want to express through word and deed that they care.

QUESTION TWO

*Is there someone who can help me get
my business affairs in proper order?*

"Special Organizational Services, Inc." (SOS)* has been established to help meet this need.

About SOS

No one wants to think about it, but with the death of a loved one, families are always confronted immediately with matters that must be taken care of in settling various business and personal affairs. In order to help families during this time of adjustment, many banks offer SOS services at no cost or obligation that can save survivors time and unnecessary confusion.

How SOS Works

At time of need, family members are invited to call the SOS bank and arrange, at their convenience, for an appointment with one of the SOS advisors. Working with a member or members of the family, the advisor will prepare a comprehensive written checklist defining the proper authorities to be notified and where they are located, certain practical measures that should be taken, and the documents and other basic information that will be required in filing claims for such benefits as:

Social Security
civil service
life insurance

---

*Ideas and materials used by permission, Mr. Bill Walker, President, Special Organizational Services, Inc., Athens, Texas.

pension plans
railroad retirement
profit sharing plans
teacher's benefits
veteran's benefits

Knowing the exact documents needed in filing various claims gives family members the opportunity to assemble data that is required and avoid repeated conferences with claims personnel at various government agencies.

(Pre-Survivor) (Post Survivor)
ORGANIZATION CONSISTS OF:

WHAT . . . documents need to be located or applied for.

WHAT . . . documents are needed to file claims.

WHY . . . these documents are needed.

WHY . . . these documents are needed.

HOW . . . these documents are obtained.

HOW . . . benefits are obtained (using copyrighted checklist).

(Pre-Survivor) (Post-Survivor)
DIRECTION CONSISTS OF:

WHO . . . to contact.

WHO . . . to contact.

WHERE . . . the offices are physically located.

WHERE . . . the offices are physically located.

WHEN . . . appointments with attorney, accountant, insurance agent are scheduled.

WHEN . . . appointments with attorney, accountant, insurance agent are scheduled.

*SOS does not replace the need for
legal and other professional services.*

In settling the business and personal affairs of the deceased, the services of attorneys, public accountant, and life underwriters are required in resolving legal matters, fulfilling accounting requirements, and in settling life insurance claims. Under no circumstances will an SOS advisor attempt to provide legal, accounting, or other professional counseling.

To assist families, SOS advisors will discuss with them areas in which the services of professionals are required and advise them of the detailed information that will be needed to proceed directly with professional counseling. This is included in the comprehensive checklist which gives a methodical review of all possible benefits and the documents and data that will be required.

SOS Pre-need Booklets

For those wishing to prepare in advance for the eventual settling of business and personal affairs, the SOS bank offers a free SOS Record of Personal Information booklet in which vital data that will be required can be entered now—while all members of the family are able to calmly contribute to organizing the details that sooner or later must be faced. The booklets are available from SOS advisors. An SOS Record of Household Items is also available for the asking.

SOS is a courtesy service

You can obtain SOS assistance, an exclusive service of the SOS bank, simply by asking for it. You do not have to be a customer of the bank. The service is free and available to anyone who needs it. If a friend or relative should die in another city, you may call your SOS bank and they will give you the name of the SOS bank in that city.

SOS has compiled a list of things to do after a death has occurred.

This list has been compiled as a guide and aid for a person who suddenly finds herself or himself in a position of responsibility after a death occurs. Everyone wants to share the burden of the people involved, but usually feels helpless as to how to proceed.

Because many deaths occur between midnight and dawn, the first ten items can be taken care of in deference to the things that must wait until the daytime hours.

1. Notify proper person in the family's church.
2. Make necessary telephone calls where travel time may be a factor.
3. Arrange for someone to spend the night with the family and give medication if prescribed by the doctor.
4. Answer and keep list of late telephone calls and/or visitors.
5. Assume responsibility for small children and arrange for them to be taken care of outside the home for a day or two (if the family so desires).
6. Check food supplies at the residence and make a grocery list (keeping in mind that food will be brought in by friends and neighbors, and probably large quantities of coffee and tissues will be needed and should be anticipated).
7. Arrange for someone to keep a careful record of calls, food, offers of assistance, and so on.
8. Ascertain condition of clothing to be needed. (Some washing and ironing may be indicated.)
9. Select clothing to be worn by deceased and take it to the funeral home.
10. Help select the pall bearers and gather information that will be needed by the funeral director for the obituary.

11. Check with SOS advisor and attorney who drew up the will for any special funeral instructions.

12. Determine which relatives are to stay in the home. Some guestroom preparation may be necessary.

13. Make additional telephone calls to family and friends. Keep a list of all calls made and the responses.

14. Schedule the appointment with the funeral director.

15. Notify employer (employees, if deceased was employer).

16. Arrange to have someone remain at the residence and straighten up during the funeral.

17. Arrange for a meeting with the attorney and insurance agent.

18. Locate all papers pertaining to the deceased, such as the will, insurance policies, and so on. Do not throw away any papers until it has been determined by the SOS advisor that they are worthless.

19. Schedule appointment with SOS advisor for complete organization and direction.

QUESTION THREE

How can I prepare for death?

The way to prepare for death is to find the real purpose of life*:

A noted physician recently said, "Medical science is giving us longer life but no reason to live."

Science cannot deal with the purpose of life.

The meaningless, frustrated, unhappy lives of many people indicate that

A

REAL

PURPOSE

FOR

LIVING

IS

LACKING.

---

*"The Real Purpose of Life." A booklet published by Max Barnett. Used by permission: For additional copies of the booklet, write to Student Office, 1141 N. Robinson, Oklahoma City, OK. 73103.

A PERSON GOES TO SCHOOL AND HE

—EVENTUALLY GRADUATES

—MARRIES

—GETS A JOB

—HAS A FAMILY

—BUYS A HOUSE

—SENDS HIS CHILDREN THROUGH SCHOOL

—CONTINUES TO WORK

—EVENTUALLY RETIRES

—DIES

Is this all there is to life? Something seems wrong. What is it?

GOD
CREATED
MAN
AND
DESIRES
TO
HAVE
FELLOWSHIP
WITH
HIM

"GOD CREATED MAN IN HIS OWN IMAGE."
—Genesis 1:27

MAN WAS CREATED WITH:

1. THE CAPACITY FOR FELLOWSHIP WITH GOD
2. A WILL (AN ABILITY TO CHOOSE)

GOD WANTS OUR FELLOWSHIP BUT HE DOESN'T FORCE US TO LOVE HIM. THE CHOICE IS OURS.

LET'S LOOK AT THE BEGINNING OF MAN'S HISTORY IN THE GARDEN OF EDEN.

God said to man, "OF THE TREE OF THE KNOWLEDGE OF GOOD AND EVIL, THOU SHALT NOT EAT . . . FOR IN THE DAY THAT THOU EATEST THEREOF THOU SHALT SURELY DIE."—Genesis 2:17

Satan said, "YOU SHALL NOT SURELY DIE . . . YOU SHALL BE AS GODS."—Genesis 3:5

Man did eat; "THEREFORE THE LORD GOD SENT HIM FORTH."—Genesis 3:23

Man was thus separated from God.

SEPARATION FROM GOD IS SPIRITUAL DEATH.

MAN
EXERCISED
HIS GOD-GIVEN
ABILITY AND CHOSE
TO DISOBEY
GOD.
THIS WAS SIN.

According to the Bible, SIN is:

1. Missing the mark—a failure to be what God created you to be.

2. A deliberate choosing to do what is wrong—rebellion against God.

3. A condition in which you are separated from God.

"FOR ALL HAVE SINNED, AND COME SHORT OF THE GLORY OF GOD."—Romans 3:23

"THE WAGES OF SIN IS DEATH . . ."
(DEATH IS SEPARATION)—Romans 6:23

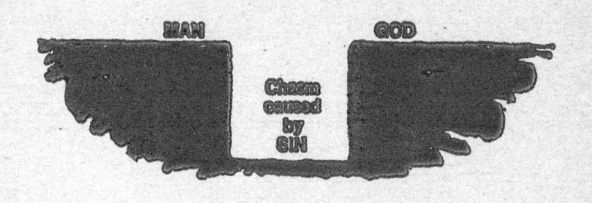

Nothing man can do of himself—good works, being baptized, joining a church, moral living—can bring him into a right relationship with God. (See Eph. 2:8-9.)

Man is separated from God and unless something happens, he will be eternally separated. "AND . . . IT IS APPOINTED UNTO MAN ONCE TO DIE, BUT AFTER THAT THE JUDGEMENT."—Hebrews 9:27

What is God's answer for man's helpless condition?

God continued to love us and sent his son Jesus Christ to die to pay the penalty for our sin.

"JESUS SAID UNTO HIM, I AM THE WAY, THE TRUTH, AND THE LIFE: NO MAN COMES UNTO THE FATHER, BUT BY ME."—John 14:6

Jesus Christ is the ONLY bridge by which man can come to God.

"BUT GOD *PROVED* HIS LOVE TOWARD US, IN THAT,

>
> WHILE
>
> WE WERE
>
> YET SINNERS,
>
> CHRIST
>
> DIED FOR US."
>
> —Romans 5:8

"FOR CHRIST ALSO HAS ONCE SUFFERED FOR SINS, THE JUST FOR THE UNJUST, THAT HE MIGHT BRING US TO GOD, BEING PUT TO DEATH IN THE FLESH, BUT MADE ALIVE BY THE SPIRIT."

—1 Peter 3:18

Although Christ died for all men, why aren't all men Christians?

Because every man must make a personal response—by faith.

BY
FAITH

YOU CAN RECEIVE JESUS CHRIST. YOU CAN INVITE HIM INTO YOUR LIFE.

"BUT AS MANY AS RECEIVED HIM, TO THEM GAVE HE POWER TO BECOME THE SONS OF GOD, EVEN TO THEM THAT BELIEVE ON HIS NAME."—John 1:12

Once Christ comes into your life he wants to be your Lord and Master and give meaning and real purpose to your life. He can do this only as you allow him to.

"AND THAT HE DIED FOR ALL, THAT THEY WHICH LIVE SHOULD NOT HENCEFORTH LIVE UNTO THEMSELVES, BUT UNTO HIM WHO DIED FOR THEM, AND ROSE AGAIN."
—2 Corinthians 5:15

"FOR TO THIS END CHRIST BOTH DIED, AND ROSE, AND ASCENDED, THAT HE MIGHT BE LORD."—Romans 14:9

LET'S SUMMARIZE...

1. God created man and desired his fellowship.

2. Man disobeyed God and fellowship was broken.

3. Jesus Christ paid the penalty for man's sin and became the only bridge by which man could come into fellowship with God.

4. You must *appropriate* what Christ did on the cross for you by receiving him personally. You can do this by:

    a. recognizing your need of him.

    b. being willing to turn from your sin—Christ can give you the power once he comes into your life.

    c. believing Jesus Christ died for you.

    d. inviting him into your life.

"FOR WHOSOEVER SHALL CALL UPON THE NAME OF THE LORD SHALL BE SAVED."
—Romans 10:13

IF
YOU
WANT
TO RECEIVE
CHRIST

YOU CAN PRAY THIS PRAYER. REMEMBER THAT BECOMING A REAL CHRISTIAN IS NOT JUST SAYING WORDS BUT RECEIVING A PERSON—CHRIST.

Lord,
I know I have done wrong.
I am willing to turn from my sins.
I believe Jesus Christ died for me.
Please come into my life and forgive me of my sins.
I receive you into my life as my Savior and Lord
as best I know how right now.
Amen.

DID YOU ASK CHRIST TO FORGIVE YOU OF YOUR SINS AND COME INTO YOUR LIFE?
DID YOU MEAN IT?
WHAT HAPPENED?

"AND THIS IS THE RECORD, THAT GOD HAS GIVEN TO US ETERNAL LIFE, AND THIS LIFE IS IN HIS SON. HE THAT HAS THE SON HAS LIFE; AND HE THAT HAS NOT THE SON OF GOD HAS NOT LIFE. THESE THINGS HAVE I WRITTEN UNTO YOU THAT BELIEVE ON THE NAME OF THE SON OF GOD; THAT YOU MAY KNOW THAT YOU HAVE ETERNAL LIFE."—1 John 5:11-13

Jesus said, "AND HIM THAT COMES TO ME I WILL IN NO WISE CAST OUT." John 6:37

Believe God and his word, not your feelings.

BELIEVING

THAT

JESUS

CHRIST

IS

THE SON OF GOD, AND THAT HE DIED ON THE CROSS, WAS BURIED, AND ROSE AGAIN THAT I MIGHT HAVE FORGIVENESS OF MY SINS AND EXPERIENCE HIS INDWELLING PRESENCE IN MY LIFE, I HAVE THIS DAY RECEIVED HIM. I DO CONFESS JESUS CHRIST TO BE MY LORD AND SAVIOR.

AIDS TO GROWTH IN THE CHRISTIAN LIFE

1. FELLOWSHIP WITH CHRIST (1 Cor. 1:9)

   a. Bible—Read the word of God daily (1 Pet. 2:2)

   b. Prayer—Talk to God daily (Phil. 4:6-7)

2. FELLOWSHIP WITH OTHER CHRISTIANS

   a. Church—Relate yourself to a church where Christ is preached and attend regularly

   b. Other Christians—Associate with them as you have opportunity.

3. PERFORM A MINISTRY IN THE WORLD (Matt. 28:19-20)

   a. Witness—Tell others of Christ (Mark 5:19)

   b. Help other Christians grow (Eph. 4:29)

   c. Serve God wherever you are (1 Cor. 10:31)

DO NOT DEPEND UPON FEELINGS.

THE PROMISE OF GOD'S WORD, NOT OUR FEELINGS, IS OUR AUTHORITY. THE CHRISTIAN LIVES BY FAITH (TRUST) IN THE TRUSTWORTHINESS OF GOD HIMSELF AND HIS WORD. THIS TRAIN DIAGRAM* ILLUSTRATES THE RELATIONSHIP BETWEEN FACT (GOD AND HIS WORD, FAITH (OUR TRUST IN GOD AND HIS WORD), AND FEELING (THE RESULT OF OUR FAITH AND OBEDIENCE).

The train will run with or without the caboose. However, it would be futile to attempt to pull the train by the caboose. In the same way, we, as Christians, do not depend on feelings or emotions, but place our faith (trust) in the trustworthiness of God and the promises of his word.

---

*Reproduced by permission. Copyright © Campus Crusade for Christ, Inc. (1966). All rights reserved.

QUESTION FOUR

I am a Christian, but I do not understand why I do not have joy and peace in my life. How can I have a meaningful spirit-filled life* here on earth?

EVERY DAY CAN BE AN EXCITING ADVENTURE FOR THE CHRISTIAN who knows the reality of being filled with the Holy Spirit and who lives constantly, moment by moment, under His gracious control. The Bible tells us that there are three kinds of people:

1. NATURAL MAN (One who has not received Christ.) "But a natural man does not accept the things of the Spirit of God; for they are foolishness to him, and he cannot understand them, because they are spiritually appraised" (1 Cor. 2:14).

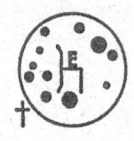

SELF-CONTROLLED LIFE
E – Ego or finite self on the throne
† – Christ outside the life
● – Interests controlled by self, often resulting in discord and frustration

---

*Reproduced by permission. Copyright © Campus Crusade for Christ, Inc. (1966). All rights reserved.

2. SPIRITUAL MAN (One who is controlled and empowered by the Holy Spirit.) "But he who is spiritual appraises all things . . ." (1 Cor. 2:15).

CHRIST-CONTROLLED LIFE
- † – Christ on the throne of the life
- E – Ego—self dethroned
- ● – Interests under control of infinite God, resulting in harmony with God's plan

3. CARNAL MAN (One who has received Christ, but who lives in defeat because he trusts in his own efforts to live the Christian life.)

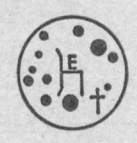

SELF-CONTROLLED LIFE
- E – Ego or finite self on the throne
- † – Christ dethroned
- ● – Interests controlled by self, often resulting in discord and frustration

"And I, brethren, could not speak to you as to spiritual men, but as to carnal men, as to babes in Christ. I gave you milk to drink, not solid food; for you were not yet able to receive it. Indeed, even now you are not yet able, for you are still carnal. For since there is jealousy and strife among you, are you not fleshly, and are you not walking like mere men?" (1 Cor. 3:1-3).

1. GOD HAS PROVIDED FOR US AN ABUNDANT AND FRUITFUL CHRISTIAN LIFE.

Jesus said, "I came that they might have life, and might have it abundantly" (John 10:10).

"I am the vine, you are the branches; he who abides in Me, and I in him, he bears much fruit; for apart from Me you can do nothing" (John 15:5).

"But the fruit of the Spirit is love, joy, peace, patience, kindness, goodness, faithfulness, gentleness, self-control; against such things there is no law" (Gal. 5:22-23).

"But you shall receive power when the Holy Spirit has come upon you; and you shall be My witnesses both in Jerusalem, and in all Judea and Samaria, and even to the remotest part of the earth" (Acts 1:8).

THE SPIRITUAL MAN—Some personal traits which result from trusting God:

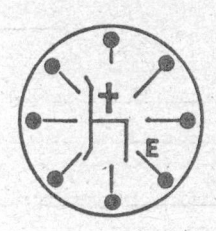

Christ-centered	Love
Empowered by the Holy Spirit	Joy
Introduces others to Christ	Peace
Effective prayer life	Patience
Understands God's Word	Kindness
Trusts God	Faithfulness
Obeys God	Goodness

The degree to which these traits are manifested in the life depends upon the extent to which the Christian trusts the Lord with every detail of his life, and upon his maturity in Christ. One who is only beginning to understand the ministry of the Holy Spirit should not be discouraged if he is not as fruitful as more mature Christians who have known and experienced this truth for a longer period.

WHY IS IT THAT MOST CHRISTIANS ARE NOT EXPERIENCING THE ABUNDANT LIFE?

2. CARNAL CHRISTIANS CANNOT EXPERIENCE THE ABUNDANT AND FRUITFUL CHRISTIAN LIFE.

The carnal man trusts in his own efforts to live the Christian life:

A. He is either uninformed about, or has forgotten, God's love, forgiveness, and power (Romans 5:8-10; Hebrews 10:1-25; 1 John 1:1-2:3;6; 2 Peter 1:9; Acts 1:8).
B. He has an up-and-down spiritual experience.
C. He cannot understand himself—he wants to do what is right, but cannot.
D. He fails to draw upon the power of the Holy Spirit to live the Christian life.

(See 1 Cor. 3:1-3; Rom. 7:15-24; 8:7; Gal. 5:16-18.)

THE CARNAL MAN—Some or all of the following traits may characterize the Christian who does not fully trust God:

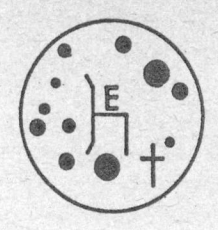

Ignorance of his spiritual heritage
Unbelief
Disobedience
Loss of love for God and for others
Poor prayer life
No desire for Bible study
Legalistic attitude
Impure thoughts
Jealousy
Guilt
Worry
Discouragement
Critical Spirit
Frustration
Aimlessness

(The individual who professes to be a Christian but who continues to practice sin should realize that he may not be a Christian at all, according to 1 John 2:3, 3:6,9; Eph. 5:5.)

THE THIRD TRUTH GIVES US THE ONLY SOLUTION TO THIS PROBLEM...

3. JESUS PROMISED THE ABUNDANT AND FRUITFUL LIFE AS THE RESULT OF BEING FILLED (CONTROLLED AND EMPOWERED) BY THE HOLY SPIRIT.

THE SPIRIT-FILLED LIFE IS THE CHRIST-CONTROLLED LIFE BY WHICH CHRIST LIVES

HIS LIFE IN AND THROUGH US IN THE POWER OF THE HOLY SPIRIT (John 15).

A. One becomes a Christian through the ministry of the Holy Spirit, according to John 3:1-8. From the moment of spiritual birth, the Christian is indwelt by the Holy Spirit at all times (John 1:12; Colossians 2:9-10; John 14:16-17). Though all Christians are indwelt by the Holy Spirit, not all Christians are filled (controlled and empowered) by the Holy Spirit.

B. The Holy Spirit is the source of the overflowing life (John 7:37-39).

C. The Holy Spirit came to glorify Christ (John 16:1-15). When one is filled with the Holy Spirit, he, too, will glorify Christ.

D. In his last command before his ascension, Christ promised the power of the Holy Spirit to enable us to be witnesses for him (Acts 1:1-9).

HOW, THEN, CAN ONE BE FILLED WITH THE HOLY SPIRIT?

4. WE ARE FILLED (CONTROLLED AND EMPOWERED) BY THE HOLY SPIRIT BY FAITH; THEN WE CAN EXPERIENCE THE ABUNDANT AND FRUITFUL LIFE WHICH CHRIST PROMISED TO EACH CHRISTIAN.

YOU CAN APPROPRIATE THE FILLING OF THE HOLY SPIRIT RIGHT NOW IF YOU:

A. Sincerely desire to be controlled and empowered by the Holy Spirit (Matt. 5:6; John 7:37-39).

B. Confess your sins. By faith thank God that He

has forgiven all of your sins—past, present, and future—because Christ died for you (Col. 2:13-15; 1 John 1:1-2:3; Heb. 10:1-17).

C. By faith claim the fullness of the Holy Spirit, according to:

1. HIS COMMAND—Be filled with the Spirit. "And do not get drunk with wine, for that is dissipation, but be filled with the Spirit" (Eph. 5:18).

2. HIS PROMISE—He will always answer when we pray according to His will. "And this is the confidence which we have before Him, that, if we ask anything according to His will, He hears us. And if we know that He hears us in whatever we ask, we know that we have the requests which we have asked from Him" (1 John 5:14-15).

FAITH CAN BE EXPRESSED THROUGH PRAYER...

HOW TO PRAY IN FAITH TO BE FILLED WITH THE HOLY SPIRIT

We are filled with the Holy Spirit by faith alone. However, true prayer is one way of expressing your faith. The following is a suggested prayer:

Dear Father, I need you. I acknowledge that I have been in control of my life, and that, as a result, I have sinned against you. I thank you that you have forgiven my sins through Christ's death on the cross for me. I now invite Christ to take control of the throne of my life. Fill me with the Holy Spirit as you commanded me to be filled, and as you promised in your Word that you would do if I asked in faith. I pray this in the name of Jesus. As an expression of my faith, I now thank you for taking control of my life and for filling me with the Holy Spirit.

Does this prayer express the desire of your heart? If so, bow in prayer and trust God to fill you with the Holy Spirit right now.

HOW TO KNOW THAT YOU ARE FILLED (CONTROLLED AND EMPOWERED) BY THE HOLY SPIRIT

Did you ask God to fill you with the Holy Spirit? Do you know that you are now filled with the Holy Spirit? On what authority? (On the trustworthiness of God himself and his Word: Heb. 11:6; Rom. 14:22-23.)

Do not depend upon feelings. The promise of God's Word, not our feelings, is our authority. The Christian lives by faith (trust) in the trustworthiness of God himself and his Word. The train diagram illustrates the relationship between fact (God and his Word), faith (our trust in God and his Word), and feeling (the result of our faith and obedience) (John 14:21).

HOW TO WALK IN THE SPIRIT

Faith (trust in God and in his promises) is the only means by which a Christian can live the Spirit-controlled life. As you continue to trust Christ moment by moment:

A. Your life will demonstrate more and more of the fruit of the Spirit (Gal. 5:22-23), and will be more and more conformed to the image of Christ (Rom. 12:2; 2 Cor. 3:18).

B. Your prayer life and study of God's Word will become more meaningful.

C. You will experience His power in witnessing (Acts 1:8).

D. You will be prepared for spiritual conflict against the world (1 John 2:15-17), against the flesh (Gal.

5:16-17), and against Satan (1 Pet. 5:7-9; Eph. 6:10-13).

E. You will experience His power to resist temptation and sin (1 Cor. 10:13; Phil. 4:13; Eph.1:19-23, 6:10; 2 Tim. 1:7; Rom. 6:1-16).

SPIRITUAL BREATHING

By faith you can continue to experience God's love and forgiveness. If you become aware of an area of your life (an attitude or an action) that is displeasing to the Lord, even though you are walking with Him and sincerely desiring to serve him, simply thank God that He has forgiven your sins—past, present and future—on the basis of Christ's death on the cross. Claim his love and forgiveness by faith and continue to have fellowship with him. If you retake the throne of your life through sin—a definite act of disobedience—breathe spiritually. Spiritual breathing (exhaling the impure and inhaling the pure) is an exercise in faith that enables you to continue to experience God's love and forgiveness.

1. Exhale—confess your sin—agree with God concerning your sin and thank him for his forgiveness of it, according to 1 John 1:9 and Hebrews 10:1-25. Confession involves repentance—a change in attitude and action.

2. Inhale—surrender the control of your life to Christ, and appropriate (receive) the fullness of the Holy Spirit by faith. Trust that he now controls and empowers you, according to the command of Ephesians 5:18, and the promise of 1 John 5:14-15.

QUESTION FIVE

*What is the difference in the way a
Christian and a non-Christian meet death?*

The attitudes and words of people approaching death reveal the great difference between Christians and non-Christians. Consider these contrasts:

François Voltaire:

This famous French philosopher, writer, and agnostic declared in health that Christianity was a good thing for chambermaids and tailors to believe in, but not for people of wisdom. Before dying, he cried to his doctor: "I am abandoned by God and man! I will give you half of what I am worth if you will give me six months' life. Then I shall go to hell, and you will go with me. O Christ! O Jesus Christ!"

John Wesley:

The founder of Methodism is credited with redirecting England from moral disintegration while Voltaire was spreading his infamous doctrines across the Channel. He logged a quarter of a million miles on horseback and preached 42,000 sermons. When he lay dying at the age of eighty-eight, he said confidently: "The best of all is, God is with us."

Napoleon (Bonaparte):

This brilliant military strategist won many battles before being decisively defeated at the Battle of Waterloo. Later, while waiting to die, he wailed, "I die before my time, and my body will be given back to the earth. Such is the fate of him who has been called the great Napoleon. What an abyss between my deep misery and the eternal kingdom of Christ."

Ann Judson:

She arrived in Burma as a missionary two years before Napoleon's defeat at Waterloo. She and her husband, Adoniram, toiled seven years before seeing their first convert. Then Adoniram was imprisoned and tortured by the Burmese king. Ann died a short time after his release. She greeted death with these words: "Oh, the happy day will soon come when we shall meet all our friends who are now scattered—meet to part no more in our Heavenly Father's house."

Paul of Tarsus:

When Paul realized that he would soon die, he told Timothy: "But watch thou in all things, endure afflictions, do the work of an evangelist, make full proof of thy ministry. For I am now ready to be offered, and my time of departure is at hand. I have fought a good fight, I have finished my course, I have kept the faith: Henceforth there is laid up for me a crown of righteousness, which the Lord, the righteous judge, shall give me at that day: and not to me only, but unto all them also that love His appearing" (2 Tim. 4:5-8).

QUESTION SIX

What can I say to someone in grief?

One of the most profound things that you can do for a person in sorrow is to be with him and communicate an attitude of your caring.

I do not remember much that was said to me when I was in deep sorrow, but I do remember who came to be with me during that time. It is important that you do not say anything negative or disrespectful. The most important thing to do is communicate in your own way so that you care for them in their time of hurt. One of the meaningful notes that I have received was from a student in one of my classes who lost his father. The note simply read: "Your attitude of 'I care' was a deep comfort to me."

QUESTION SEVEN

Where are the dead right now and what are they doing?

Men through the ages have sought some tangible proof of immortality. Job cried out: "If a man die, shall he live again?" (Job 14:14). The resurrection of Jesus is the answer to the agelong cry. Christ's resurrection declares that death is not the end of life for the Christian. He has life with Christ beyond the grave.

2 Corinthians 5:1-8 states that to be absent from the body is to be present with the Lord.

> For we know that when this tent we live in now is taken down—when we die and leave these bodies—we will have wonderful new bodies in heaven, homes that will be ours forevermore, made for us by God himself, and not by human hands. How weary we grow of our present bodies. That is why we look forward eagerly to the day when we shall have heavenly bodies which we shall put on like new clothes. For we shall not be merely spirits without bodies. These earthly bodies make us groan and sigh, but we wouldn't like to think of dying and having no bodies at all. We want to slip into our new bodies so that these dying bodies will, as it were, be swallowed up by everlasting life. This is what God has prepared for us and, as a guarantee, he has given us his Holy Spirit.
>
> Now we look forward with confidence to our heavenly bodies, realizing that every moment we spend in these earthly bodies is time spent away from our eter-

nal home in heaven with Jesus. We know these things are true by believing, not by seeing. And we are not afraid, but are quite content to die, for then we will be at home with the Lord.

"Soul sleep" is not scriptural. This concept was a medieval philosophy which is not consistent with the Word of God. There is consciousness after death. Luke 16:19-31 gives an account of consciousness after death.

"There was a certain rich man," Jesus said, "who was splendidly clothed and lived each day in mirth and luxury. One day Lazarus, a diseased beggar, was laid at his door. As he lay there longing for scraps from the rich man's table, the dogs would come and lick his open sores. Finally the beggar died and was carried by the angels to be with Abraham in the place of the righteous dead. The rich man also died and was buried, and his soul went into hell. There, in torment, he saw Lazarus in the far distance with Abraham.

" 'Father Abraham,' he shouted, 'have some pity. Send Lazarus over here if only to dip the tip of his finger in water and cool my tongue, for I am in anguish in these flames.'

"But Abraham said to him, 'Son, remember that during your lifetime you had everything you wanted, and Lazarus had nothing. So now he is here being comforted and you are in anguish. And besides, there is a great chasm separating us, and anyone wanting to come to you from here is stopped at its edge; and no one over there can cross to us.'

"Then the rich man said, 'O Father Abraham, then please send him to my father's home—for I have five brothers—to warn them about this place of torment lest they come here when they die.'

"But Abraham said, 'The Scriptures have warned them again and again. Your brothers can read them any time they want to.'

"The rich man replied, 'No, Father Abraham, they won't bother to read them. But if someone is sent to them from the dead, they will turn from their sins.'

"But Abraham said, 'If they won't listen to Moses and the prophets, they won't listen even though someone rises from the dead.'"

The scriptures do not present specific data regarding what the redeemed are doing right now as they are present with the Lord. Perhaps the first great activity is the worship of God. Revelation 19:1-8 is a scene of worship in heaven. Many of the well-known passages in the Psalms relate to the worship of God in heaven. Read Psalm 29:9, 95:6, 96:9, 132:7. Read also Hebrews 1:6.

Many parts of the New Testament reveal the ultimate fellowship that the believers will have in heaven. Read Hebrews 12:23, for example.

One of the greatest things about heaven is that the former things are passed and the dead are in God's presence right now!

QUESTION EIGHT

How do I tell children about death?

A child should not be told in detail the things which he cannot understand. Rather than being evasive, modify the explanations to the child's level of understanding; however, parents should answer a child's questions about death directly and honestly.

The following are some negative perspectives which should be avoided: (1) Avoid stories and fairy tales about death. (2) Do not give the child an explanation that you cannot accept yourself. (3) Avoid any interpretations which may backfire and cause the child to reach conclusions which have not been intended.

Children must be told the truth. It is more disturbing for a child to think that his grandmother has left him to go live with God than for him to realize that she died of a disease she did not want and fought bravely to overcome.

Many over-protective parents, in their haste to save their children from all unpleasant things, try to protect them from pain and grief. A child should not be deprived of his right to grieve. He should be free to grieve in the loss of someone he loved.

We do not have to tell all the brutal facts but we must be honest in telliing children about death. They can handle truth better than falsehoods. Children should be allowed to remain children even though they must be spoken to frankly and honestly.

When a death occurs, and a child is not told the truth about what happened, he may become confused. Anxiety soon fills his mind and he fills his knowledge gap with figments of his imagination far more bizarre than the truth would be. Childhood fantasies can be carried into maturity.

Perhaps the question may arise of what to tell your children when they see you crying during the grief process. When our mother died, my sister related that each time she would weep, her children would become very upset and also cry. It scared the children to see their mother sorrow openly. She explained to her children that we are happy that Mom is in Heaven with Jesus, but we miss her here on earth now. That is why we cry.

The resurrection of Jesus gives us a new way of looking at the experience of death of a loved one. When we lose someone through death, the issue at stake is really a matter of time, not a matter of being.

All grief comes back to one thing—we run out of time. In terms of time and space we are separated, but this is not final. Our losses are real but not permanent. Death is an interruption in relationships. Therefore, grief is running out of time, not running out of love and relationships.

This is not to infer that our family relationships will be continued in the same social structure that we have here on earth. In Heaven we will know each other and have fellowship, yet we will be members of one large family of God.

QUESTION NINE

What about a definite terminal illness?

Sorrow and grief may be more easily borne if prepared for in advance. The refusal to accept foresight of death may increase the shock and could contribute to a later refusal to face the fact of death.

If an individual knows in advance some of the reactions to expect in grief, he will not treat his normal behavior as if it were abnormal. The "real show" is very different from a "dress rehearsal," but it is also very different from what it could have been if it had not been rehearsed.

Ask the Lord for strength to bear the events. Talk with others who have had experiences similar to those you are currently facing. Stay in a mental meditation of scripture. "Thou will keep him in perfect peace, whose mind is stayed on Thee" (Isa. 26:3). "Precious in the sight of the Lord is the death of his saints" (Ps. 116:15).

The time approaching death can be the most meanngful contribution that we make to others during life. For in dying, you may teach someone how to live—and how to die.

QUESTION TEN

Where can I find help in the bible when I have a time of need?

These quick references in scripture will be a significant aid in helping you find resolutions to many of the needs that you may have while in the grief process.

When you are facing grief:
    2 Corinthians 1:3-5
    2 Corinthians 5:8
    Romans 8:26-28
    Philippians 1:21

When you have lost your sense of worth, value and dignity:
    Psalm 139

When you are feeling inadequate and weak:
    2 Corinthians 12:9-10
    Philippians 4:13

When you are feeling depressed and lonely:
    Romans 8
    Psalm 23
    Hebrews 13:5

When you are in need of forgiveness:
    1 John 1:9
    Hebrews 4:15-16

When you are not controlled by the Holy Spirit:
    1 John 2:15-17
    Philippians 4:8
    Psalm 106:13-15

When seeking inner serenity and peace during a time of turmoil:
>   Isaiah 26:3
>   John 14:27
>   John 16:33
>   Philippians 4:6-7

When you need to conquer your fears:
>   2 Timothy 1:7
>   Psalm 27:1

When you need courage:
>   Ephesians 6:10-13
>   Psalm 138:3

When you are suffering afflictions:
>   1 Peter 5:10
>   1 Peter 4:12-13
>   Psalm 34:19
>   2 Corinthians 4:17

When your patience is being tried:
>   James 1:2-4
>   Romans 8:28-29

When you are facing temptations, decision making, and are needing wisdom:
>   James 1:2-6
>   James 1:12-15
>   1 Corinthians 10:13

When you desire guidance:
>   Proverbs 3:5-6
>   James 1:5

When your problems are getting you down:
>   Psalm 55:22
>   1 Peter 5:7

When you are tired, weary, and in need of strength and rest:
>   Isaiah 40:28-31
>   Galatians 6:9
>   Matthew 11:28-30

When you feel that you are being treated unjustly:
    1 Peter 2:19-23
    1 Peter 4:12-15

When you are facing failure:
    Romans 8:28-29

When you are facing danger and needing protection:
    Psalm 23
    Psalm 91
    Psalm 121

When you have doubts about your salvation:
    John 3:16
    Romans 10:9-10
    1 John 5:11-13

When you have doubts about God's keeping power and your eternal security:
    Romans 8:38-39
    1 Peter 1:5
    Philippians 1:6

When you desire provisions for life's basic *needs*:
    Matthew 6:33

When you are worried that your sharing of God's Word is of no avail:
    Isaiah 55:11

Conclusion

You have finished this book. What have you read? You have been confronted with some questions and answers about death and the grief process. Now you have several alternatives: (1) you may continue to dwell on your grief in a morbid way; (2) you may continue to feel sorry for yourself; (3) you may continue to make other people miserable; or (4) you may find a new normal life and help others because of your experience.

In your grief, you have been going through a deep experience. It has not been an experience which you wanted, but one which has resulted in painful truth about life and death. This truth has brought about the reality that we do not know how to live until we know how to die!

Grief behavior may take one of two forms. One way may be a matter of facing up to what has happened and accepting it. The other form of grief behavior results in retaining problems, refusing to work them out, which causes other problems to occur.

Expression of grief is therapeutic! These factors are extremely important:

1. Admit to yourself how you feel and what you think.

2. Talking is important, yet,

3. It has to be aloud to someone who cares for you.

How do you help people who are in the grief process? Perhaps you telephone, go to see them, send flowers, donate money to a meaningful cause, invite them over to your home once or twice to show that you care, and then you slip back into your own routine life assuring yourself that you have done all that anyone could do. THAT IS NOT ENOUGH! A person in grief needs you desperately. To effectively help someone demands an understanding of the grief process, a willingness to listen, and a lot of time. Become involved in that person's life and help with any areas in which assistance may be needed. Most of all, be a genuine friend who communicates that you care. Most of the time, the funeral is not the end of the grief process; it is only the beginning.

In the process of learning how to live and die, there are certain factors about our behavior which are frightening but normal. If we treat our normal feelings of grief as if they are abnormal, our mind short-circuits; thus, guilt and frustration result. We must treat normal *human feelings normally*!

Most important, you may find power in the Christian faith that you did not realize was there until you put scripture to work in your life. It is through the Word of God that you will find a faith stronger than death! Because you now have some deeper insights into the normal grief process, you will now be better able to communicate with a person in grief.

Diagram of Grief Process

GRIEF PROCESS

DIAGRAM OF EVENTS FOR SURVIVORS

- ANTICIPATED
- UNANTICIPATED
- Point of DEATH of Loved One

CHRISTIAN
- REPRESSION
- GUILT
- SHOCK
- PANIC
- WEEPING
- PHYSICAL DISTRESS
- RESENTMENT
- DEPRESSION

Position of HOPE in Christ.
- ACTIVE — Resources are experientially in Christ.
- PASSIVE — Reactivate fellowship with God.

NON-CHRISTIAN — Depends on acts of humanity & rationalization.

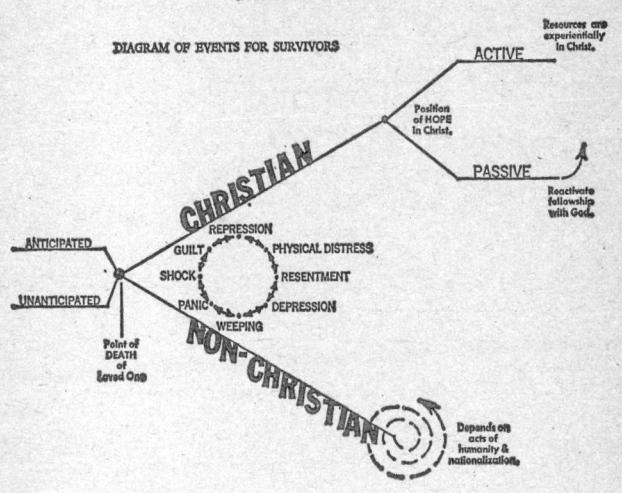

Whether anticipated or unanticipated, the death of a loved one causes both the Christian and the non-Christian to go through a grief process in adjustment to the loss. The Christian makes his adjustment by making his daily experience synonymous with his position in Christ. For the non-Christian there is a tendency to be dependent on humanistic solutions and rationalization.

Definition of Terms

Christian	A person who has an established relationship with God through His Son, Jesus Christ (Rom. 10:9-10, John 3:16, 1 Tim. 2:5-6).
Death	Physical death—Separation (transition) of body and spirit resulting in decay of the body (Ecc. 12:7).
	Spirit death—Separation of the spirit from God, resulting in the ruin of the spirit (2 Thess. 1:8-9).
Defense mechanism	Type of reaction designed to maintain an individual's self-image (concept) of adequacy and worth rather than to acknowledge and cope directly with the stress or sorrow situation.
Depression	Emotional state of dejection or despair and feelings of worthlessness and apprehension.

Emotion	Expression of one's deep feelings. Emotions cannot be separated from situations or experiences which evoke them. Emotion is an inside thermometer which is affected by outside events.
Empathy	Ability to understand and to some extent share the state of experiences (mental, physical, emotional, spiritual) of another person. (See *sympathy*.)
Faith	Confidence in God and His ability to guide and provide for the individual's needs (Heb. 11:1-6).
God's Word	God's thoughts revealed to man through the Bible. The revelation of God's actions with His people throughout the ages, particularly through His Son, Jesus Christ (2 Tim. 3:16).
Grief Process (Death)	A series of thoughts, feelings, and actions during a period of adjustment to the loss of a loved one.
Guilt	A feeling of having committed a breach of conduct. Guilt comes when one does not meet what he expects of himself as well as what others expect of him.
Heaven	Eternal presence with the Lord God. The final dwelling place of the Christian is known as Heaven (John 14:2-3, Rev. 21:4).
Hell	Eternal absence from the Lord God. The final dwelling place of the non-Christian is called hell (Mark 9:48).
Hope	An expectation toward attaining an equilibrium in that all things

	work together for good for those who love the Lord and are trying to fulfill His purposes (Rom. 8:28).
Life	Physical life (life before death)—The period of duration of a person in the earthly physical body. Spirit life (life after death)—The life when a Christian is absent from the body and present with the Lord God.
Normal Behavior	Relative to the expected behavior (behavioral expectation).
Panic	Sudden, severe, overpowering fright involving intense anxiety.
Prayer	Communication with God. The offering of adoration, confession, thanksgiving, and supplication to God (John 16:24).
Repression	Means by which intolerable memories are kept out of consciousness.
Resentment	The feeling of indignant displeasure because of something regarded as wrong.
Shock	A blow, impact, sudden agitation of the mental or emotional senses.
Sin	Anything according to scripture that interferes with an adequate relationship with God through His Son Jesus Christ.
Sorrow (death)	Mental and emotional suffering or sadness that arises from the loss of a loved one.
Sympathy	An association or relationship between people so that whatever affects one, similarly affects the other or others. Sympathy emphasizes pity rather than awareness

	of the state of another person. (See *empathy*.)
Trust	Assured reliance on God with confident hope (Heb. 11).

Suggested Reading

Adams, Jay E. *Competent to Counsel.* Nutley, New Jersey: Presbyterian and Reformed Publishing Company, 1973.

Allen, Charles. *When You Lose A Loved One.* Westwood, New Jersey: Fleming H. Revell Company, 1959.

Brown, H. C. *A Search For Strength.* Waco, Texas: Word Books, 1967.

Drakeford, John W. *Counseling For Church Leaders.* Nashville: Broadman Press, 1961.

Edman, V. Raymond. *They Found the Secret.* Grand Rapids: Zondervan Publishing House, 1960.

Frankel, Victor. *Man's Search For Meaning.* New York: Washington Square Press, 1963.

Graves, Charles B., Jr. *When Tragedy Strikes.* Dallas: Crescendo Press, 1973.

Jackson, Edgar Newman. *Understanding Grief: Its Roots, Dynamics and Treatment.* New York: Abingdon Press, 1957.

Kubler-Ross, Elisabeth. *On Death and Dying*. New York: Macmillan, Inc., 1970.

Lewis, C. S. *A Grief Observed*. New York: Seabury Press, 1961.

Lewis, C. S. *Mere Christianity*. New York: Macmillan Inc., 1960.

Marshall, Catherine. *To Live Again*. Westwood, New Jersey: Fleming H. Revell Company, 1957.

Marshall, Catherine. *Beyond Our Selves*. New York: McGraw-Hill Book Company, 1961.

Phillips, J. B. *Your God Is Too Small*. New York: Macmillan, Inc., 1961.

Vernon, Glenn M. *The Sociology of Death*. New York: Ronald Press, 1970.

Westburg, Granger E. *Good Grief: A Constructive Approach to the Problem of Loss*. Philadelphia: Fortress Press, 1972.